GODMA

Owen Ifill, MD

Karibbean Kumfa
P u b l i s h e r s

Karibbean Kumfa Publishers
2192 Fulton Street, Brooklyn, NY 11233
Visit our website at www.KaribbeanKumfa.com

Cover design and text layout by Grafixwerks Design
Visit their website at www.Grafixwerks.com

Illustrations by Johnathan Azore.

REVIEW OF "GODMA" by Owen Ifill, MD

"GODMA", a rather skillful play on the word "dogma" to suggest the absolute power of God, who could be male, female or an object, is the title chosen by Owen Ifill, MD, for the second collection in which he continues his ongoing conversation with himself while on his journey of self-discovery and self-empowerment. The poet himself describes this work that contains some one hundred and twenty-three untitled selections in the following way:

It is a chronicle of things that bother,
amaze, amuse, perplex and fascinate me.
It asks questions and suggests answers;
it laughs
it cries
it breathes
and it dies.
It ultimately
is life
seeking to know itself.

The last two lines, however, undoubtedly identify this work as universal in appeal. The reader is not only swept along in the current of self-awareness as the poet communicates unique insights into the human mind, but is also inspired to seek his/her own answers to many of the issues discussed in this philosophically engaging exploration of a variety of life experiences. These include love, the existence and absolute belief in the power of God, human existence, creation, values, war, discrimination, prejudice, dreams, and involvement among others.

Of varying lengths, most of the untitled poems in this book are conversational or anecdotal in tone and readily fit into the description of "poenecdotes", a term coined in 1980 by one of the poet's Guyanese friends to describe this kind of writing. The first poem is one of many in which he skillfully utilizes such a tone through direct address and illustrates his attempt to encourage his readers to seek comfort in their belief in God. This, he argues, will bring back one's perspective. This, for him, is GODMA:

And when,
from time to time,
you become depressed, torpid,
and confused;
when you feel isolated;
when you feel an emptiness and meaninglessness
….

At such times,
raise your head
and caress the skies.
Take deep, full breaths
of God,
and your perspective will return.
This,
is GODMA.

Brief selections that focus on specific issues and reflect the poet's
thoughts on a variety of issues are also included. They seem, in other
words, like words of wisdom. Two poignant examples are seen in the
second selection on page 18 and in the last one on page 25: "Failure/is
not an outcome./ Failure / is the judgment of an outcome" (18); "A belief/
is actually a device/ to abolish doubt" (25).

Technically, the use of everyday language is further proof of the appeal
to everyone, and, at the same time, adds to the note of sincerity that per-
vades the collection. The reader often feels that he/she is on the same
quest as the writer and shares his depression, his anguish, his confusion,
his joy, and his comfort among other emotions. The repetition of key
words/phrases is also extremely effective in communicating his feelings
and responses. The writing is further enhanced by appropriate illustra-
tions of Johnathan Azore, a Guyanese artist. Some of them are strategi-
cally placed to differentiate the untitled selections. However, a charac-
teristic feature of the style is the liberal use of some punctuation marks,
especially the comma and semi-colon. This, most likely, effectively com-
municates the manner he wishes to convey the messages of his pieces.
One can contend, though, that in the more contemporary sense, the
rhythm and flow of some pieces would have been more effectively
attained with less frequent use of these typographical symbols.

There can be no doubt, nevertheless, that readers who love this kind of
poetry are certainly going to be engaged in a treat of "deep" or "heavy"
contemplation of life and should endeavor to secure a copy of GODMA,
which is soon to be released by Karibbean Kumfa Publishers, a Guyanese
owned publishing agency in Brooklyn, New York.

Reviewer: Roslin A. Khan, Ph D
Asst. Professor, Caribbean Literary Scholar
& Newspaper columnist

Other Works by Owen Ifill, MD

Infinite Circles

In Flux

Buxton Rising (Producer)

Illustrations by Johnathan Azore.

Godma
Is a book
which is actually the continuation
of **Influx** a previous publication.
It is essentially an ongoing conversation
with myself.
It is a chronicle of things that bother,
Amaze, amuse, perplex and fascinate me.
It asks questions and suggests answers;
It laughs;
it cries;
it breathes;
and it dies.
It ultimately
is life
seeking to know itself.

This book is dedicated to Des, Jes, Buxton, and Kashibunga and soulja Tambrin. You have all played a significant role in the birthing of this document. Love Ya.

And when,

from time to time,

you become depressed, torpid,

and confused;

when you feel isolated;

when you feel an emptiness and meaninglessness

that you cannot name,

and for which there is no apparent cause;

when you have become

a creation of pubs, porsches, politics,

prejudice, power, people, pride, property, polemics,

perversion and pretense,

pain prevails;

for perspective is perturbed.

At such times,

raise your head

and caress the skies.

Take deep, full breaths

of God,

and your perspective will return.

This,

is GODMA.

Those
who legislate drug laws;
who send addicts to prison
for no good reason;
who spend unheard of millions,
to stop
what they do not even
seek to understand;
And if you do not even understand
what you seek to change,
how can you ever change it?
It is the riddle of a fool.
And those who do this,
are more addicts
than those they seek to punish.
They are addicted to the position
that they are right.
They are addicted to the notion
that theirs'
is the only viable solution,
even when faced
with the truth of its failure.
They are addicted to the conclusion
that admission of failure
is worse than failure itself;
And admission of failure
necessarily demands a new approach;
But they are addicted
to the old.
They fear newness.

All totalitarian systems
will fail;
without fail.
They will fail
because their architects fail;
They fail
to see,
that people
are not some abstract concept
to which all encompassing rules apply.
They fail to see,
that inflexible rules
stifle individuality
and doom creativity.

The Murder of a man
for the murder of another man,
which in modern parlance
is called capital punishment;
is at least as sick
and as criminal
as the crime in question.
Maybe even more;
for some have killed
in the grips of rage and passion.
Our killing of these people,
is done with premeditation,
and in cold blood.

And a woman came;
a woman,
distraught beyond reason;
her brow bedeviled with a pain
her spirit could not hide.
And the questions;
they fell out of her,
a jagged torrent, between sobs and rigors.
What is love?, she railed;
Does it even exist?, she wailed;
and if it does, where is it?,
What is the criteria for its visit?
Where is it?.
Show me the shit!!!.
Why, after a life of struggle, sacrifice, and pain,
must my reward be more struggle and more pain?
Where is the love?
Where is this God they speak of?.
And the old one looked up;
the one of the gray and matted hair;
the one,
whose beard had forgotten to stop growing,
and had become enmeshed and confused
in his equally graying pubic hairs;
And this was obvious,
for he wore no clothes.
He wore his nudity the way the children did;
with aplomb;
without shame or modesty;
matter of factly.
And he looked up,
saying nothing;
just staring,

for that interminable minute, or so,
at God knows what;
for his eyes were blank and unfocused,
as they always seemed to be.

He always seemed absent,
yet there was a mysterious presence;
an empty house
with god in it;
a vacant lighthouse
with a lamp lit.
And that divine madness
shone forth from his empty eyes;
and he said,
in that loud whisper
that is barely audible,
yet clear as the bell that calls the young skittish ones
out to school.
And he said;
Who is love,
and what is God?,
And where do they live?,
and are they really any different
one from the other?.
These are questions that no one
can answer for you.
The answering of these questions
is your life's work;
and once answered,
there are no other questions.
But let me humor you,
for that is all I can do here.
Love and God are one;

ever existent and irrefutable;
and you, incidentally,
are its proof.
You are both the love manifested,
and the love
that made that manifested love, possible.
You are both this and that;
Chit and sat;
and yet you are more,
for you are also the process
that bridges them.
Where is the love?
It is here,
ever present;
its manifestation is everywhere.
It is the mother breastfeeding her child.
It is the mother,
the child,
the breast,
and the milk,
and it is the subtle and soothing dynamic
that binds them.
It is all of the above.
It is the completed circle.
It is the unity of all things.
And yet it isn't,
for love means infinitely more than I can communicate.
It is the father patiently teaching his son
the mechanics of a jump shot,
while cleverly camouflaging
the life wisdoms he seeks to impart.
It is the father, the son, the game and the wisdom,
and it is the unspeakable give and take

that renders the process worthwhile.
It is all of the above.
It is the completed circle.
It is the unity of all things.
And yet it isn't,
for love means more than can be said or postulated.
It is the man walking his dog,
and it is the dog walking his blind man.
It is a tree reaching for the sun,
and it is the sun saying, here I am,
have all of me;
I am thee.
It is evil and good,
and the place where they meet, and chat;
for it is only at this place
can you see their true meaning
and significance.

It is the alpha and the omega,
and what joins them.
It is everything.
It is everything,
yet it means nothing until you know it;
until you live it;
until you are it.
As I said,
and as I am again now saying;
all I have said
is really meaningless;
it is to humor you;
to lighten your burden,
for love ultimately means
what I can never say.
It is a game,

so its meaning is in its play.
Go forth therefore,
and play like your life depends on it;
for it does.

One of life's great paradoxes,
is that the things with the most value,
have no value.
For something to have value,
it must have utility
and it must be limited.
Air,
and God,
for example,
have no value;
they both have utility,
but they are ubiquitous.
They are limitless.

Why is it
that most outdoor games,
and a few indoor ones,
I might add,
are played with balls?.
What is it about balls
that we find so fascinating?

And he sat with the couple
who were to be married;
And he said to them;
As of today
you are to quit using the words
I LOVE YOU;
for you have no clue
what they mean.
After you've lived together for,
say, ten years;
after countless fights;
after break-ups and make-ups;
after jealousies and judgments;
after anger, hurt and disappointment,
you probably will have an idea
what love does,
and does not mean.
And you will come to discover a strange phenomenon.
You will come to discover that,
when you come to know what those words mean,
there is no longer any need
to use them.
Your actions will speak them.
Your laughter will leak them.
Your lovemaking
Will reek,
of things you couldn't speak.
Until then,
if you use those words,
you would be lying to each other.

We live
in two interlocking dreams.
We dream in sleep,
then wake up into another dream,
which we call reality.
The dream which we call reality,
is only more convincing
because it appears concrete,
and we seem to have at least some control
over its workings.
Ours is a cycle of dreams,
in a state of endless and intoxicating sleep.

And then there comes that day.
That day,
when it becomes clear,
crystal clear,
that your life;
that which you were living;
makes no sense,
has no tense,
lacks coherence;
is fraud and pretense,
and hence,
is fear and defense.
On that day,
of its own accord,
is born a presence;
a subtle
and profound intelligence;
a singular reverence
for all you sense.
And above all,
there is the silence.
Yes,
the silence.

Talkin bout dem guys;
the ones with the alibis.
The ones that live on highs,
on lies;
those guys.
The ones always seein pies in the skies,
and never reaching dem;
always preachin dem.

Talkin bout dem dudes;
the ones with the attitudes;
The ones who diss sistas
at the drop of a hat,
and think that that's phat;
and think they're all that;
All what?
All chat;
All rat-a-tat.

Talkin bout dem dogs;
The ones who walk dogs
and don't know their kids.
The empty drums
with no lids;
the inverted pyramids;
the mental invalids.
Those kids.
Those clueless hominids.

Talkin bout dem fools;
The ones who believe that jails are schools,
and guns are tools
that somehow makes you cool.

The ones that hold down corners 24/7,
and ain't doin nutten,
and ain't sayin nutten.
The ones who talk to hear themselves,
who wouldn't dare
to dare themselves.
The professional victims.
Always bitchin.

Talkin bout dem playaz;
The ones who abuse sistaz
to feel good about themselves;
who wouldn't turn a straw
to redeem themselves.
The ones who hate on brothas
cause they're livin progressive;
whose whole outlook
is dark and negative.
The ones
with chips on their shoulders,
heads full of boulders,
and feel the world owes them something.

Talking bout dem guys;
The ones with the alibis;
The ones that live on highs,
on lies,
those guys.
The ones always seein pies in the skies,
and never reaching dem.
Always preachin dem.

There are no absolutes
in the area of human behavior.
That is a given.
So why is it that we are demanding just that,
in the arena of human sexuality?
If all humans were heterosexual,
that would actually be an anomaly.
That would not be normal.
That would not be normal
because there is no other area of human behavioral dynamics
to which we all conform absolutely.
Homosexuality, therefore,
is actually normal behavior.
It is normal because it conforms to the relative nature
of all behavioral practices.

It isn't so much
that people change,
as it is
that peoples' perspectives change.

And even though
my contribution may be worthless seeming;
Even though
who I am,
what I do,
and who I share my life with,
will never be news;
this much I know.
I am at least as important
as the most important human
who has ever lived.
The world could not be,
without insignificant me.
Whoever you may be,
your equal
is me.

The children
of great people,
are usually ordinary people.
If great people knew the source of their greatness,
even if they did not want to share it with their spouses,
would they not tell it to their children?

The term sitting on the fence,
has been given a black eye
for no good reason.
The fact is,
the fence sitters
have the greater perspective;
have the wider view;
for they can clearly see the pastures
on both sides.
Their choice,
if they ever choose to choose,
will at least be more rational
than their grazing counterparts.

Failure
is not an outcome.
Failure
is the judgment
of an outcome.

Evolution and creation
as we characterize them,
are both myths
of concrete minds;
for if life is eternal;
if life is beginning-less and endless,
how is creation relevant?
and if time, chronological time,
is really mind gymnastics;
is really
sleigh of psyche,
on what foot does evolution stand?

There is a saying
where I come from.
The saying is,
"Bush gat ears".
Americans are now learning it.

For greatness,
was never meant to be
a measure of individual achievement.
Greatness is a function of how,
once one has achieved,
one uses that experience and that prominence,
to cause others to achieve.
Greatness is measured
by how many other greats you spawn;
by how many other lights
you turn on,
before you are gone.

Guilt is such a pervasive
and sinister energy;
it can make you feel guilty,
for not feeling guilty.

To live consciously
is to see the contradictions you live,
while knowing
that you are,
and forever will be,
beyond contradiction.
It is to love those who hate;
For it is to know
that those who hate,
are people who live a kind of fearful dream;
a dream from which,
if they were to awaken,
they would see
that who they hate,
is really themselves.
It is to accept who you are,
whomever that may be;
for without acceptance of your current circumstance,
how can you grow beyond it?

It is common and appropriate,
for science to sometimes answer a question,
with another question.
Politics however,
takes the cake.
Politics can answer a question
without even bothering
to address the question.

Those who say
that money is the root of all evil,
give money a bad name.
There was evil
before money was invented.

History only continues to be relevant
because we keep reliving it.
If we really learned from our history
and demonstrated that in our lives,
then history
would really be history;
we could forget it.
If you have learnt from,
and corrected a mistake,
what is the value of remembering that mistake?.
How is it relevant?
It is just water under the bridge.

We all wax poetic
about the virtues of our blackness,
while we all seek fame and fortune
to escape the prison
of our blackness.

People can only hurt people
when they cannot see,
that who they are really hurting
is themselves.

Love
does not question;
for if love questioned, theorized,
and ultimately concluded,
then love
would not be love;
Love would be logic;
Love would be science.
Love does not, and cannot question,
for where love lives,
questions are never born;
Love knows all.

The concept
of God the creator,
is both inaccurate and inadequate.
God
is creator,
created,
and the process by which,
and through which creation proceeds.
God is the baker,
the ingredients,
the oven,
the bread,
and the process of baking itself.
God is creation.
The ALL of it.
And so God is/is not.

A belief,
is actually a device
to abolish doubt.

Musicians, like people,
are basically of three types;
those who learn the rules,
and live by,
and in them;
these are the mediocre majority,
whose music is a perpetual echo;
nothing new.
And there are those
who learn the rules,
so they can break them.
These are the innovators
and trend setters;
the avant garde.
Then there are those
who never even bother
to learn the rules.
They brought them
with them.
These are the prodigies, savants,
and geniuses.

DINA SAX

Why is it
that we give scant thought
to the origin of thought?.
Is it because thought inherently seeks
to not examine itself?;
for thought beginning to examine itself
is the birth of wisdom;
for thought becomes transparent;
for thought begins to wither,
and to die,
when wisdom begins to grow.

All of the great wisdom teachers;
All of the great pedagogues
of life,
have essentially taught
energy management.
Energy generation, conservation,
or assimilation;
or a combination of them.

The perpetuation of anti-Jewish sentiment in America,
is predicated on circumstances
that nobody wants to discuss.
There is, I believe,
a popular perception
that Jews have disproportionate wealth,
and hence disproportionate power;
and hence disproportionate influence.
There is also,
a perception that Government is more sympathetic
to Jewish causes and issues,
with their attendant privileges and their own rules.
This, I believe,
is the result of a historic guilt complex
that haunts humanity's conscience;
this,
coupled with the fact that opposing Jewish causes
is seen as political suicide.
Political careers have suffered
for voicing similar concerns;
and they are,
I believe, legitimate concerns.
Even among the general public,
there is this irrational anxiety to breach this issue in public;
for you are an anti Semite
if you are critical of anything Jewish.
The if-you-tell-a-Jew-his-yarmulke-is-too-tight,
you-are-an-anti-Semite-syndrome.
And dissent that cannot be expressed
becomes resentment.
And so Governments and politicians,
and Jews themselves,
actually help to perpetuate anti-Jewish sentiment.
and then they wonder
where it all comes from.

Social commentators who are comedians
have to be unfulfilled people.
I suspect that the comments they make,
they want to publicly make,
but comedy is used as a vehicle
to blunt the edginess of the message.
They seek to give
a serious laugh.
What actually happens,
is that they get a laugh,
but not the last one.
People always laugh;
people, however, get so lost in the laughter,
that they lose the message.

Politicians can be classified
according to their angle of fork;
fork of the tongue,
that is.
The more successful the politician,
the wider the angle.
Acute angles
are small town boys.

The standard
that we should hold ourselves to;
is speaking out,
if not doing so would or could,
cause or perpetuate harm or suffering to others,
or to ourselves.

Blacks claim African motherhood
as if
she were exclusive to them.
African motherhood,
is humanity's motherhood.
African motherhood
is seminal motherhood.

One of the many miraculous abilities of women,
is their ability to say nothing for hours,
while talking on the phone.
They can be silent
while talking.

Discrimination is necessary
for perception as we know it,
to be possible.
It is the cornerstone of perception.
We perceive
because we discriminate,
and not the other way round.
And experience is not possible
outside of perception/discrimination.
So,
we all discriminate,
for we all perceive and experience;
we are all breaking the law.

My writings
are conversations
with myself.
I am talking to myself;
And occasionally,
as you will notice,
I even answer myself.
That makes me a nut, I'm told;
and nuts are seeds.
They should not be taken seriously.

I hear all the time
that there are no stupid questions;
that all questions are legitimate.
I beg to disagree.
There are, in fact, stupid questions.
There are dumb questions.
Stupid questions
are questions that are not asked, to inquire;
they are asked questions,
the answers to which
the questioner already knows.
He seeks to showcase his knowledge.
You will know him,
for his signature is this;
he always adds to, amplifies,
or goes into more detail than the speaker,
on a topic or point on which he is supposedly
not very knowledgeable.

Like truth,
opinion needs neither defense
nor justification.
Truth is its own defense,
and its own justification.
Opinions on the other hand
are beliefs.
They are not truth.
They are changeable.
They are free to change,
or be changed,
with new experience and knowledge;
with our projection beyond our prejudices.
To defend an opinion,
is to defend the ephemeral;
is to defend the subjective;
and to justify opinion
is to waste energy.

Science answers questions,
with questions;
Politics answers questions,
without answering them.
Religion
doesn't even entertain them.

If the world was perfect;
If it was
as most hope it would be;
No politics or persecution;
No crime, no corruption;
No religion, no division.
No discrimination, no competition.
No war or worry,
No hate, no hurry.
No might is right,
No black, no white.
No poverty, hunger or disease;
No fat cats with all the cheese;
No isms, no schisms,
No drugs, no prisons.
If our world was perfect, the truth is,
we would all probably commit suicide;
And why?
Because there'd be nuthin
to f--kin
do.

We are all schizophrenics;
we all have many faces.
We are all different people,
to different people.

Chronic diseases
are unexpressed emotions;
are unexpressed frustrations;
are unexpressed anger, pain and fear.
Chronic diseases
are sick energies,
made flesh.

Total belief, faith,
will, and intent,
are one and the same;
for if you have faith in something,
you totally believe in it;
and if you totally believe in something,
you will it;
you intend it.
It is made flesh.
It is so.

Is thought a product of brain?
Does brain emit thought,
the way suns emit light?;
the way children emit life and laughter?
the way nature emits love?
Are brain and thought one and the same?,
the way sun and light
are one and the same?
the way children and life are one and the same?
the way GOD and LOVE
are one and the same?
In the absence of brain,
is thought possible?
Does a dead man tell no tales
because he thinks no tales?
Or is brain an antenna?;
a super complex one;
one of extensive surface area
and unmatched circuit wizardry.
One that retrieves thought
out of the virtual expanse of space/time.
Is thought therefore,
an independent entity?,
that swirls and drifts and eddies
around and through us.
A dead man therefore tells no tales,
not because the tales are not there,
he just isn't receiving them.
Or is brain both a transmitter and receiver?
It is,
and yet it isn't thought.
Or is it neither of the aforementioned?
I have come
to not fear answering a question
with another question.

This may sound crazy, my child,
but there was a time;
a time before any of us could collectively remember;
a time,
when politics made sense;
it just wasn't called politics;
a time,
when genius meant simplicity,
and beauty was a feeling
and not a decision.
This was the time
before the advent of wars;
for people could neither see their reason,
nor their justification.

He,
who has all the answers,
knows the least.

It is rumored
that in the beginning;
in that time
when God created the heavens and the earth.
In that period,
after SHE made the animals,
and birds, and plants,
and bacteria and viruses and all such;
and after HE beheld it,
and said it was good,
decided to make man;
and did.
But God reasoned,
if God was openly accessible to man,
like air,
man would not appreciate it;
man would take God for granted.
So God decided to hide from man.
IT surmised,
that if man had to search,
to navigate,
to investigate,
then he would better appreciate.
God was at the time walking down a beach,
for it is at deserted beaches, deserts, and mountaintops
that God does its thinking.
And he saw lucifer sunbathing,
dark glasses and all,
with a smile on his face.

And so he stopped and engaged him.
He told him what he planned,
and where he would hide;
under the sea.

And Satan laughed;
that shrill, singular, and sordid laugh.
You underestimate
the power of your creations, he said;
man, in time, will figure it out;
no doubt.
You don't know that devil called man,
he said; you'll find out.
Why don't you hide inside of him instead?
In his heart, in his head.
There he would never think to look.
And it was God's turn to laugh;
that booming, yet still and silent
musical singularity
that was his laugh.
How about if I were to be everywhere?, IT mused;
both inside and out;
both north and south.
If I were to be in everything,
and to be everything
at the same time,
how could he find me?.
For that which is ubiquitous
is not only invisible,
but existent / nonexistent.
If I am at once the seer,
the eye,
the mechanism of sight,
the light which makes vision possible,
and that which is perceived,
how could I be found?
And satan laughed, again.
That is plain dumb, said satan.

How could man not find you if you are in all places,
at all times?
That, said God, wistfully,
is the question.

The Israeli/Palestinian conflict
is very instructive.
It is a great teaching tool,
though its lessons will most likely be learnt
by future generations;
we are deaf, dumb, and blind
to what it is saying;
both to us,
and about us.
What does it say,
when religion is its root,
and politics is its perpetuation?

All spiritual paths;
all devices;
all practices,
lead to your center.
And once the center is found,
then all paths become irrelevant.
You now need a ladder;
for it is here
that ascension begins.

Contrary to popular belief,
racism has nothing
to do with race.
Racism
has everything to do
with judgment.
Racism
is a psychological issue.
If all men were black,
or white;
given our current psychological constructs,
there would still be racism.
We would just call it by another name.

The idealist,
in reality,
is a realist;
for reality
is made of dreams.
The idealist knows
that reality
is really dream composition.

Art
is really a translated feeling.
Artists translate feelings, thoughts and visions,
into music, film, books, paintings etc.
The great artists
are the ones who translate the most clearly;
whose language
is the most lucid;
whose colors
are the most lurid.
They are the ones
who reproduce the feeling they felt,
in their audience;
that feeling,
which is made physical,
through art,
in turn evokes that selfsame feeling in the observer/listener.
The wonder and awe of great art
is the captured feeling
of its artist.

Your life
proceeds from you;
it is not happening
to you.
All in it,
is a result of your doing,
or not doing.
You are cause.

And so,
the questions I ask
have been asked a million times.
The truths I declare
have been said millions of times,
in millions of ways.
Nothing here
is new.
The confusion you notice,
and the longing;
that visceral longing
which you no doubt sense,
is by no means novel.
It has a history.
A history
as old as time,
and as new as life.

And how do you explain a world,
in which the reason for politics,
is people;
and the reason for poverty
is to a large extent,
politics.

You hear all the time,
people declaring
that they are proud
to be American, or Guyanese, or British, or Buxtonian,
or black, or whatever.
I can understand one being proud of some achievement,
but being proud of your place of birth
or race,
is just too much.
Being black, or Guyanese, or American
was not our decision,
so that pride is evidently misplaced.
We had nothing to do
with where we happen to have been born,
and to which race.
It would seem
that being proud of our parents,
would make more sense;
for they gave us our race
and our nationality.

You teach
what you seek to learn.
What you know
is not teachable.

I have no problem
with those who oppose abortion,
and either adopt those children,
or contribute,
not just financially,
but are presences in these childrens' lives.
The ones
that I have a problem with,
are the fanatics;
the self righteous ones;
the ones for whom the issue
is neither life nor children.
The issue is them.
These are the ones who would kill
to defend their point of view;
who would take a life
in the defense of an idea,
and not see the glaring contradiction.
These are the same ones,
who see nothing wrong
with these same children,
later dying of disease or starvation
in their mother's arms.

For life and death
are but aspects
of the self-same reality.
They are hence ONE.
The way love and hate
are but polarities
of the same energy system;
and hence complement, support,
and give reality and vitality
to each other.
The way
up is really down,
and evil and good
are really a cosmic handshake,
with a wink and a smile.
There are,
really and truly,
no opposites in reality.

This drive by science
to make people live longer;
What exactly
does it mean?
What is the purpose of living longer,
if all it adds to your life
is years?

If current trends continue,
in the next fifty years or so,
women will occupy the seats of power
the world over.
Women are becoming
more and more educated,
and more and more independent;
and their male counterparts
are dropping out more and more,
and becoming more and more dependent.
Yes,
women will rule the world.
I personally
Have no problem with that.
If it means cat fights
instead of wars;
I'm all for it.

If, as some believe,
truth has a price;
with what currency
do we pay it?

The exclamation
"Holy shit!",
was probably coined
by a guy,
or gal,
who needed to make
an emergency dump (number 2),
while at church on a Sunday.
He/she rushed into the chapel toilet,
and after relieving him/herself,
stretching, and wiping the cold sweat
from their brow,
proceeding to the toilet tissue dispenser
and finding nothing.
"Holy shit"!,
indeed.

Whenever you open your eyes;
Whatever you observe,
and whatever you experience
is an aspect of yourself;
for you created it.
If you love it,
keep doin it.
If you don't,
simply change it.
That is all.

"Accidents",
are by no means accidental,
and "coincidences"
are never coincidental.
These are terms
that have meaning
only to those who cannot see
the big picture;
to those who believe
that events, circumstances and experience
are phenomena that just happen;
that are independent of us.

He who becomes conscious
of his humility,
has lost it.
He can no longer be humble.
It is like the child
who becomes conscious
of its nakedness.

There are indeed two sides to a coin,
but we often forget the edge.
The edge
is what joins the sides;
the edge
is what makes the sides possible;
yet we often forget the edge.
It is on that edge
that life happens;
it is on that insignificant
and subtle edge,
that night and day meet,
and kiss,
and laugh
into misty dawns.
On that edge
is life's address.
Life lives
on that edge
that we hardly notice,
much less acknowledge.

We damage our children
when we reward them
for "good" behavior.
Good behavior for us,
usually means
obeying our mandates and decrees,
not answering back,
and not questioning our authority.
And so we end up raising children
who as adults,
obey blindly,
never question,
and fear authority.

Rap music
is a cornucopia of wisdom,
artistry, genius,
anger, sexism,
defiance, misogyny,
bullshit, materialism
and egomania
all rolled into one.
Rap
is all things.

And so, it seems at least,
that wars will forever be;
for it seems we will never see,
that wars
are part of the reason for wars;
that wars
sponsor themselves;
that wars
create hatred;
that wars
create anger;
that wars
create resentment;
that wars
create poverty and powerlessness,
and hence create the fuel
for further wars.
And seeking to end a problem
by sponsoring its cause,
if is not insanity,
at least is ignorance.

The phrase
"seeing is believing",
is a profound truth
whose meaning has been largely trivialized.
Thought creates our world;
both on a micro,
and a macro scale;
both in our personal lives
and our global lives.
our beliefs are what create
and color our lives.
what we believe therefore,
is what we see.
there is no other way.
seeing therefore,
is believing.

And so my child,
even though this may sound contrary
to all you've been taught,
listen me out.
Have no fear of the devil;
in fact, forget the devil.
be always watchful, however,
for "God";
for in our history
more evil has been done in the name of "God"
than the devil can even dream
to begin
to fathom.

When mad people seem to be laughing with themselves,
they in fact
are laughing at us.
They are aware
that realities are many;
and further,
that they are all probable
and relative.
The madman knows
that we are just living another version of "madness"
which we call "reality".
The madman's joke
is on us.

All delinquency
is a child pleading for help;
is a child saying,
"I am here, see me!".
is a soul
seeking refuge.
Delinquency is a symptom
of societal disease.
The degree of delinquency in a society
is a direct measure of a society's health/sanity.

Inherent in every problem,
is its solution.
A large part of every problem
is its identification;
put another way,
a significant problem with every problem,
is seeing there is a problem
and then isolating the problem.
And half the work is done.
The rest
is just worrying it;
like a shaky tooth.

If you do not accept all of you,
how can you change part of you?
If there is a part of you that you deny;
that you think ugly and shameful,
and hence needs to be hidden and repressed,
how can you change it?
If you disown it,
it grows in the cellar.

And us;
the those and them,
who have grown tired of life
but fear death,
and so live in a world
that is essentially a vice.
A vice
that tightens with time;
that has no rhythm;
that has no rhyme;
a mistake;
a cosmic crime.

I have often wondered
about a word
used mainly by American politicos.
The word is un-American.
After deliberation, study, and deep contemplation,
I have come to the conclusion
that that word
means impossible;
for it usually describes an act
done by an American
that Americans are incapable of doing.

So us;
the blacks of this world.
Let us give up the blame game,
for it's a lame game;
it's the same game
that keeps us where we're at,
on the mat.
Give it up!
Give it up;
for self pity
cannot grant power;
for broken dreams cannot flower.
for truth will never cower.
Rise
from the dust that made us;
discard the images they gave us;
let go of the negativities
that enslave us,
for only we
can save us.
Give it up!

There are gifts
that a friend cannot give to you.
I speak of those gifts
that only the enemy can deliver.

This all consuming malaise,
that lifts boots in unison
and bends minds out of shape,
will continue;
for hearts are no longer where they used to be;
at the heart of things.
Hearts now languish underfoot
in deserts
of dead consciences;
but hearts are hearts,
and will and must continue
to make connections;
for hearts must return
to the heart of things.

If you hadn't looked
it wouldn't have mattered;
nothing mattered at the time.
But you looked,
and you looked again;
and you called something
out of the heart of me.
And it came;
a slow, staggering drunk
that was blinded by the light
it had never seen;
but it came;
and I saw it;
and I felt it;
but I didn't know it;
had never seen it;
and it made faces at me
and danced a weird jitterbug in the sunlight.
You never told me what it was,
that genie,
that came out of me;
and it never came back to say.
But tell me,
why does the world seem so different now,
and why does my face smile
when I'm not looking?

Dreamt I saw you
walking on naked feet;
dreamt I saw you
walking on a flaming, jagged street,
in some scarred place.
Dreamt I knew you
from some life;
some forgotten life;
but you didn't know me,
for your eyes said it
in their subtle slant.
Dreamt you were me,
but somehow
that couldn't be;
I just wasn't privy
to that strange beauty;
that cataclysmic choreography;
I didn't fit
in that celestial scenery.
but I knew I loved you,
in some life;
in some forgotten life.
I felt it,
deep inside
of you.
And so,
touch my hand through time,
and walk me backward
through flaming jagged streets
into old sunsets,
so we can find what was.
Show me eternity
in this life.

Women's attraction
for bad boys,
lies in their realness;
their authenticity;
their audacity.
It lies in their unabashed expression
of their feelings
and their impulses;
without regard,
or care, for that matter,
for who is watching.
Bad boys
dare to mock society.
Bad boys are forever saying,
"look at me!;
I am real!
And women like that.
After all,
who can resist
that which is real;
that which is authentic;
that which
is truly itself.

Mouth meets mouth,
languid and leisurely
on an unerring course;
fleshy crescents merge
and eclipse.
Vipers rave and rant
behind bars,
sweating their slime
in mouthfuls.
Bars open,
and they meet
in no man's land.
The duel begins
in which none shall win;
as fortunes shift
unerringly;
until the victor
is the vanquished,
and the vanquished
is king.

The word "IMPOSSIBLE", is,
to my mind,
one of the most powerful words
in our language.
It has power
because we believe in its implications.
In reality,
it is a meaningless word.
It is a foolish concept
that we have allowed
to control and shape our lives.
Impossibility
is a lie;
It is a monumental lie
that we have given to ourselves
because we are too mentally lazy
to question its premise.
The word "IMPOSSIBLE",
is an expletive;
It is an insult
to all humans everywhere.
It should be banned
from all our vocabularies.

How can our civilization be serious?;
how can our history
and its "truths" not be trivialized,
when Hitler, for example,
is a villain,
and Columbus
is a hero?

I remember once,
while working on my manuscript,
my daughter,
who was a toddler at the time,
grabbed a few pages and tore them up.
And I laughed,
for I got the joke.
It was God saying,
"Enough of these nonsense words;
Walk your talk".

What I did
was unforgivable,
so I'm asking of you the impossible;
to forgive me.
I discovered
that in betraying your trust,
I betrayed myself.
The hurt you now feel,
believe me,
I feel the double of it.
I hurt for you
and I hurt for me.
And I love you.
Please allow me
to demonstrate who I can be;
to find the good
that I know is inside of me;
for I am
not what I did;
I am more,
much more;
Allow me therefore,
to show you....... please.
Friends?

And so,
one day I came to this realization;
this strange realization;
this alien
and frightening realization.
I discovered
that the parts of me
that I detest;
that I deny;
that I am not willing to accept in myself,
are exactly what I cannot stand
in other people.
The people I cannot stand,
mirror the aspects of me
that I cannot tolerate.
They show me the caged monster
that I have hidden
in the cellar.

The anti-terrorism policy,
is a fear based initiative.

Most of us
live our lives
as though it were an exam;
An exam
that is set by,
and graded by our society;
an insane exam,
that is both Arbitrary and pointless.
And the hapless few
who are unfortunate enough
to pass it,
they lose their lives.

There are two fundamental reasons
why you shouldn't burn bridges.
One is,
that you may need it to cross
on your way back.
The other is,
that you could do serious time;
for that
is called terrorism these days.

Grounded people;
People who have encountered themselves;
People who know
what authentic power is,
and from whence it comes,
make poor politicians.
This is so
because their opinions are theirs;
Their opinions
are extensions
of who they are.
They do not wave
with the polls,
or the rolls
of green stuff.
Their convictions are theirs,
and do not bend
with bad press,
and the rest.
They have no past,
and hence
cannot be compromised.
They can be blacklisted;
Never blackmailed.

I was in a bank one of those days,
and I saw an infomercial;
The ones they play
while you wait in line.
It essentially was saying,
that your quality of life
was the difference between your income
and your spending.
If income is high
and spending is low,
you have a great quality of life,
and vice versa.
The problem with this model is,
you can scrimp all your life
and maintain a great quality of life,
while never having a life.
And you can take that
to the bank.

Material success
is the result
of a confluence
of desire,
of focus,
and of action.
And what of opportunity,
you are no doubt wondering?.
Opportunity
is the culmination;
is the natural result;
is the creation,
of this union.
Opportunity proceeds
from the meeting
of this triad.

Society's evolution
is due in large part,
to the unraveling of the myths,
the fears,
and the ignorance,
of the majority.

For death, after all,
is a part of life;
the way an arm,
or a leg
is part of a body.
Death
is life's asshole.
It is that place
through which life relieves itself,
in order to make space
to continue the creative process.

We fear debt
in almost the same fashion
as we fear death.
It seems,
we see debt
as a kind of death.
The truth is, though,
debt, like death,
is unavoidable.
When death knocks,
you will be
in debt.

Compassion is born
out of understanding.
We;
All of us;
are capable
of anything we have ever judged
and condemned in another.
We;
all of us;
are capable of the most heinous crime
ever committed to date.
The potential;
the seed,
is in all of us.
We are all made
of the same stuff.
And Until this is recognized,
compassion is not possible.

For to hold a concept
or mental picture, steadily,
in your mind;
to constitute it clearly
and comprehensively;
to totally encircle
and contain it,
is to birth it;
is to,
in that present singularity,
create it.

Women
are strange beings;
and wives?
Wives are female people
who make it their life's work
to fix men;
to put them right.
They are always tinkering.
Wear this;
do this;
be that.
They even enter your head
to mess around with stuff.
And when the man is fixed,
the project is over;
then she loses interest,
for there is nothing else to do;
then she leaves him
for he is no longer himself;
He is her creation
which she now resents.
He is no longer authentic.
She leaves him
for a man she cannot change.
A man who keeps her busy
on the job.

And so, Buxton;
even though
your youth have gone blind,
and your mothers cannot see,
for weeping.
Even though violence and fear
poison the land;
even though
those who speak for us,
do not even know us;
even though today is dark
and tomorrow is nebulous,
we know that reality is plastic;
that change
is law;
that tomorrow holds
whatever it is
that we deeply desire of it.
We know,
that peaks always follow valleys,
for it can be
no other way;
for that,
is the way of things.

Even if,
as is claimed,
Castro has taken political prisoners;
has executed political opponents;
Even if
he denies "freedoms"
of his own people;
while none of the above is justifiable,
why is there never any mention
of those he has helped to liberate
in Africa and the Third World?
Why is there no mention
of those he helped to educate?;
Why is nothing said,
about the walking dead
that have benefited
from Cuban health
and humanitarian aid?.
And what of the training of third world professionals?.
Why, I wonder,
is nothing said?
I would like to think
that it is not because these lives
are not important;
that it is not because these people
are black,
or brown;
But I wonder.
And this is the dishonesty
that makes laughable
the continued U.S. policy
toward Cuba.

The man
on the weird hill,
Looked,
and saw,
and couldn't comprehend.
He had been looking
for a long time,
For his "space" was timeless;
ageless.
He saw people going nowhere
and getting there fast;
real fast.
He saw people going somewhere,
And never getting there;
never ever
getting there.
He saw people
eating hell for breakfast
and eating more hell
for dinner;
pure hell.
He saw people bathing in heaven,
when heaven
is scarce like hell.
The man on the hill,
on the weird hill,
saw
People patronizing people;
People parasitizing people;
People persecuting people;
People pissing off people;
People who wanted to know people;
People who wanted to be people;

People who weren't people;
People who believed
in the people
in people;
People becoming people,
and people who had to be people
for people to realize
who they were supposed to be,
simply people.
The man on the weird hill,
saw hate hiding around corners
and in tall buildings,
and he saw love
watching from across the street.
He saw bitterness
in the best of places,
and he saw strange sweetness
amongst savage squalor.
The man on the hill,
on the weird hill,
saw men die
for men who didn't deserve to live;
He saw children
who shouldn't know,
but did,
and he saw men
who should know,
but didn't.
And he looked
at the drama;
The strange funk;
The give;
The take;

The love;
The hate;
The shock;
The countershock;
fascinating game
of chess,
on wheels;
rough wheels.
The man on the hill,
on the weird hill,
smiled;
He smiled
a puzzled frown.
The man on the weird hill
is still smiling
a puzzled frown.

Democracy
Is not a noun;
It is a verb.
It is a process;
It is ever becoming.
If it ever stops becoming,
then it becomes a noun.
Then it dies.

Imperfection
is a myth;
for if we are all imperfect,
then imperfection does not exist.
Then imperfection
is perfect.

If, after writing a book,
then revisiting it after awhile,
you find nothing
you either want to modify,
to delete,
to reconstruct,
or to totally scrap,
it means you have not grown.
It means you are living
in your past;
it means
you have died.

If time,
the cosmic nuisance,
is taken out of the cause and effect equation,
then cause
is effect;
Then cause
and effect
are one and the same;
Then action and reaction
are not equal
and not opposite;
they are complementary faces
of one event.
They are one complete action.

One of my patients came to me
a few months ago.
And she said;
"Doc, my sister died; did you hear?".
"Yes", I said, "sorry about that".
"It was the crack cocaine". "They said it ruptured her heart;
and imagine, you spoke to her about it
just the other day".
"Doc, whoa!, that thing scared the shit
out of me;
I stopped using crack;
for a week or so, anyway".

To some extent,
it is our "imperfections"
that give us our individuality.
It is our individual "faults"
that make us unique.
If we were all "perfect" people,
we would all be clones
of each other.
You,
would be me.
Ain't that disgusting?

And a poor and destitute man
came to see him;
And he asked,
Why is life so unfair?
Why is it
that only the rich
can enjoy the fine amenities
of this life?;
why is it that the poor
are doomed to a life of insufficiency
and unhappiness,
while the rich are happy
and fulfilled?
Why is this so?

And he smiled,
The wise one, that is;
And he said,
after wrinkling his brow
and seemingly looking over the horizon.
This may seem weird to you,
but you chose poverty;
You chose your current condition.
You create your reality
in much the same way
as an artist creates a painting,
or a musician creates a song.
Your life situation, therefore,
is your creation;
You, at some deep level,
desire that it be that way,
whether you consciously realize it
or not.
You can change it anytime, if you wish,
by seeing the way you think,
and changing the way you think.
Life circumstances
only appear to be thrust upon you.
The truth is,
you put them there,
and you can remove them
whenever you so wish.
That, however, doesn't concern me
as much as something else you said.
You seem to think
that poverty and happiness are incompatible,
and that affluence
is synonymous with happiness.

If you believe, as you do,
that affluence brings happiness;
when you become rich
and it doesn't surrender happiness,
then you become more miserable.
So, a miserable poor man
becomes a doubly miserable rich man;
And you want to know what happened.
This is the reason for some of the suicides
that you hear about in millionaires.
They are,
by and large,
no more happier than you are;
And you, at least,
have something to hope for;
to live for.
He has attained what you crave,
and he has seen that that is not the answer.
So,
where to turn?
If money is what you want,
then simply do as I suggest;
See, look at,
how you think about money,
and you will discover
that you are who is responsible
for your poverty;
then change it.
If however,
it is happiness that you seek,
I suggest you look no further;
For it is with you 24/7.
You cannot run from, hide from,

or escape it.
It is more intimate than your shadow,
more innate than your body,
and more immediate
than your mind.
It is not dependent
on any external circumstance
or any internal drive.
It is you.
The irony of this is,
if you find who you really are,
you would be so deliriously happy
that you would laugh at money
even as it is being thrown at you.
Take your pick.
And the poor man stood there,
frozen in anger,
and he spat on him,
the wise one, that is.
And he said, before walking furiously away;
that, is total bullshit;
You are nothing but a fraud,
a hypocrite.
I came here for help
and all you do
is blame me for all my misfortunes.
And the wise one smiled,
that knowing smile,
as he wiped the mottled mucus
from his matted mane.

In Guyana,
where I happened
to have been born;
and I suspect,
in most of the third world;
Our parents;
those of the previous generation,
keep saying that the youths of this,
the current generation,
have no respect for their elders;
that our generation,
the one of their children,
was different.
They have, to my mind,
confused respect and fear.
We feared our parents;
we did not respect them.
Respect necessarily entails a relationship
of mutual regard;
a framework within which
both have the freedom
to be themselves,
and to express themselves
without fear of ridicule
or rancor.
In our relationship with our parents,
we could not have opinions,
much less express them.
We could not question
that with which we disagreed.
We were denied those rights.
The expression of those freedoms
in the youths of today
must therefore seem like disrespect.

There is a dangerous philosophy
being peddled
in America.
It is by no means new.
It has existed
from the dawn of "civilization".
It is a philosophy,
that in practice
has never proven true;
never had a clue.
It has always flattered,
to deceive.
It says
that war can end war;
that wars
are winnable;
that hate can be conquered
by anger and fear,
as if they are any different.
It says
that peace is that period
during which you are preparing for another war,
while resting up from the previous one;
during which you lick your wounds
and cultivate resentment and hate
before storming the other gate.
It says
that love, empathy, understanding and grace
have no place
in human international affairs.
It says that jingoism and nationalism
masquerading as patriotism
are not only okay,
they are the truth and the way.

In essence,
it says that history and experience are meaningless concepts,
for it blatantly ignores their lessons.
It says that we either do not have the will, the courage,
or the intelligence
to explore another way;
to greet a new day;
to call a new play.

Part of the reason
for our disagreements
and our rancor;
for our jealousies,
our hate,
and our anger,
is that we think
in black and white;
in wrong and right;
while truth lives
somewhere in the midway;
in the shades
of grey;
in laugh;
in play.

There are things
that I know,
that I don't know
how I know;
yet I know
that I know them.

Physical laws,
Are not absolute.
they are all relative.
they are assumptions
with which most of us agree.
They are hence,
not inviolable.

The collective black problem,
is one problem.
It is neither an economic, political,
or social problem.
It is a psychological problem.
Our problem
proceeds from our beliefs
about ourselves as a people.

For when God is "found",
it is often the case
that people ask themselves,
how in the world could I not have seen?
how the hell, could I not have known?;
for God, you see,
is now seen in everything.
In the sky,
in the fly,
in the toddler
waving bye.
in trees,
in a sneeze,
in a mischievous
summer breeze.
in sun,
in rain,
in hurt,
in pain;
in love
and in hate,
in your enemy
and in your mate.
in the high and the low,
in the come and the go.
God laughs,
God cries,
God lives,
God "dies".
All is God.
and this again,
is Godma.

Convention and orthodoxy
are thought of as monuments
to be preserved
and commemorated.
For them to serve us,
though,
they should be seen
as sandcastles.
You build them,
and when they have outlived their utility,
then you destroy them;
being careful to preserve
what good is still there;
in this case,
the sand.

A guilty plea,
is the admission of an error;
is the acknowledgment
of a mistake.
How is judgment,
and punishment,
relevant?

Watched you for a while,
while tossing balls
in my mind.
Asked you for a dance,
in the soft smoke;
and you
said
no,
while you sipped
your sherry.
You were beautiful,
but that's not the point.
You said no;
Why?
What's a dance?
Dance is love
in action;
fleeting,
flowing,
fluid action.
Yeah!,
dance is love.
Dance is free;
dance belongs to nobody.
Dance has no obligations,
no laws;
dance is
what we can never be.
Dance is freedom
in its purest form;
the genuine article;
the real Mccoy.
Dance

simply
is.
Dance lives in the present,
there simply
is no past.
So why won't
you dance?
Dance,
and be.
Feel yourself,
know yourself,
love yourself.
That is dance.
Dance
is your tribute
to all that is;
so forget me;
Dance
and be.

The concept of sin
is a monumental contradiction.
The only "sin"
there really and truly is,
is judgment;
for all other "sins"
proceed from judgment.
Judgment therefore,
is the parent of all "sins".
To murder, steal, hate,
or bear false witness,
you first
have to judge.
The inherent contradiction
is the following;
to call an occurrence a "sin",
is to "sin".
To call a "sin", a "sin",
is to "sin";
and why?
because calling an occurrence
or event a sin,
is to judge it
and deem it bad or undesirable.

And this talk;
all this rhetoric
about destroying and ending insurgency,
is a lie so insidious,
even its proponents believe it.
Is it then a lie?
Insurgency, by whatever name
you choose to call it,
has always existed.
Insurgency lives
wherever there are haves,
and there are have-nots;
insurgency thrives
wherever and whenever,
the rights of one are ignored,
or blatantly disregarded
by the other.
Insurgency will never die,
until we can agree
to disagree;
until we understand
that compromise is better than conflict,
and that human life
is infinitely more important
than national pride
and philosophical concepts.
Until we realize
that ours is just another way;
that there is no "right" way,
then insurgency is here to stay.

It is not with sex, my child,
that I have a problem;
for sex
is as natural
as the seasons.
It has its place;
it has its reasons.
How can I ever fault sex,
when you are its fruit?;
when it is one of the many
and glorious expressions
of truth.
No,
with sex I have no quarrel.
It is with unsafe sex
that I have a difficulty;
it is thoughtless sex
that confounds me;
for this is a grave irresponsibility,
the consequences of which,
I am not sure
you can foresee.
This, my child,
is the era of HIV.
I know
that you are at that age;
the age of flightiness, impatience,
and experimentation;
the age
of raging hormones
and sexual obsession;
but;
always think of you,

before you do
what you do;
for only you
can be responsible
for you;
taking chances
will not do.
And so,
go;
and if you remember
none of what I said today;
if you choose
to walk the other way;
know,
that ultimately
whatever you choose to do,
or not do,
your grandma
will always love you.

The anti terrorism response,
is fear sponsored.
All the signs are there.
The fingerprints
and bloodstains are there,
clear,
for all to see.
There is war;
for fear in its paranoia,
attacks perceived monsters,
and even creates them.
There is secrecy,
for fear believes that openness
is weakness;
that openness
invites attack.
There is arrogance;
for fear hates rebuke,
and interprets dissent and disagreement
as threatening and alien.
And there is myopia;
for fear in its blindness,
creates more and more laws,
with which to protect itself
and with which in fact
it drowns itself.

It's as if
it's a black thing;
all this stuff;
all this dark stuff.
This mayhem;
this misery,
this mindlessness.
It's as if it's ours,
this mud;
this dark mud,
of drugs,
of death,
of deprivation.
It's as if
we're married to it;
this dark mojo,
this bleak curse;
of fatherlessness;
of failure;
of futility;
of fruitless fantasizing.
It's as if
it's a black thing;
the self denial;
the nihilism;
the strange suicide.
How do we cure this thing?;
this dark disease.